Wrestling
Greats

# BRUNO SAMMARTINO

**Ross Davies**

**The Rosen Publishing Group, Inc.**
**New York**

Published in 2001 by The Rosen Publishing Group, Inc.
29 East 21st Street, New York, NY 10010

Library of Congress Cataloging-in-Publication Data

Davies, Ross.
Bruno Sammartino / by Ross Davies. — 1st ed.
p. cm. — (Wrestling greats)
Includes bibliographical references (p.   ) and index.
ISBN 0-8239-3432-2
1. Sammartino, Bruno, 1935—Juvenile literature. 2.
Wrestlers—United States—Biography—Juvenile litera-
ture. [1. Sammartino, Bruno, 1935– 2. Wrestlers. 3.
Italian Americans—Biography.] I. Title. II. Series: Davies,
Ross. Wrestling greats.
GV1196.S26 D38 2001
796.812'092—dc21

                                        00-012712
Manufactured in the United States of America

# Contents

Bruno Sammartino was once a world wrestling champion.

# The Legend of the Living Legend 1

In the 1960s and 1970s, Bruno Sammartino was known to wrestling fans around the world as the Living Legend. He was the greatest wrestler in the world—the strongest, too. His reign as the World Wide Wrestling Federation's (WWWF) world heavyweight champion stretched from 1963 to 1971, and then again from 1973 to 1977. He defended the title over a thousand times. Until Hulk Hogan came along in the 1980s, no wrestler was more loved or well-known than Sammartino.

But the real story of Bruno began long before he became famous. It started in the small city of Pizzoferrato in central Italy. That's where Bruno was born on October 6, 1936. His full name was Bruno Laopardo Francesco Sammartino. His parents were Alfonso, a blacksmith, and Emilia, a house-wife. Bruno was the last, and the biggest, of their seven children. He weighed eleven pounds at birth (most infants weigh less than nine pounds at birth).

The family lived in a stone house and raised food in the fields. When Bruno was only two months old, his father left home for the United States. He planned on making

One of seven children, Bruno Sammartino (second from right) was born and raised in Pizzoferrato, Italy.

money in Pittsburgh, Pennsylvania, then returning to Italy and building a bigger business so his family could live better. But when World War II started, ocean routes back to Italy were closed. Alfonso couldn't get home and the rest of the Sammartinos couldn't get to the United States. Alfonso worked in the coal fields and steel mills around Pittsburgh. He barely made enough money to send back to his family.

When Bruno was five years old, he met Giovanni Batista, a great Greco-Roman wrestler who had won a bronze medal in the Olympics. Greco-Roman and freestyle are different types of wrestling. In Greco-Roman matches, athletes may not attack the legs of their opponent; they can only attack the upper body. In freestyle matches, they may attack both.

Batista loved children and often let them train with him. Batista encouraged young Bruno. "Keep your interest, Bruno, and someday you will be champ," he told him.

Life in Europe wasn't easy in those days. World War II had broken out, and the Germans were marching through Europe. In 1943, Nazi troops arrived in Pizzoferrato. "The SS [Nazi] troops came into our town, and I'll never forget when it happened," Bruno said in a magazine interview.

"It was the middle of the night. I thought I was having a nightmare. I could hear many noises outside that woke us all up. Me, my mother, and other family members were frightened as we heard shooting. Finally, an uncle came into our house and yelled, 'Leave the town! The Germans are here and they're shooting up the town.' My mother panicked. We were told to dress quickly, grab some blankets, and then we left the house and ran. Everyone was running. The whole town. A lot of people were badly hurt or killed. Those of us who were lucky made it to the mountain. It was about a day and a half climb. As everyone scattered to different hiding places, the Germans scattered too, getting some of us while others hid. We stayed in the mountains until some of the older men came and built us a fortress out of trees. This was our new home, so it seemed."

The Nazis invaded Bruno Sammartino's hometown in 1943.

The mountain was called Villa Rocca. Later, a man allowed the Sammartinos to live in his small cabin on the mountain until the German occupation ended. Those were dangerous and difficult times for Bruno and his family. They wore rags and suffered from malnutrition. Every day they heard bombing down in the valley. Bruno tried to convince himself that he was safe, but war raged all around him.

They had no food. A few times a week Emilia Sammartino would climb down the mountain at night and sneak back into the village. "She would sneak back into the basement of our home and get food we stored there," Bruno recalled. "It would take her about two days to get back to us. In the meantime, we starved. In the winter, we actually survived by eating snow. In the summer, we ate dandelions and water."

Meanwhile, Bruno's father didn't know whether his family was dead or alive. He had heard on the news that the Germans had occupied his town back in Italy and that many people had been killed. Alfonso Sammartino was just about certain his family was dead. He had no way of getting in touch with them, nor they with him.

Life in the mountains was rough. There were no doctors. Many people became sick. Bruno's sister, Anitta, and brother, Sandrino, both died of malnutrition during the fourteen months the family spent on Villa Rocca.

The war finally ended in 1945, and the family came down from the mountain. Bruno was so sick that his mother had to carry him all the way down. When they arrived back in Pizzoferrato, they were amazed and sickened by what they saw. "The Germans left dead bodies laying around," Bruno recalled. "It was a nightmare. Bodies were all over town."

Bruno's father finally got in touch with his mother. Emilia told Alfonso there wasn't much use coming back to Italy because things were so bad in their town. Alfonso decided to bring his family to the United States. After the war, however, strict limits had been set as to how many people could enter the United States.

In 1948, the family was going to leave for the United States, but Bruno got sick and nearly died. He had caught pneumonia and lost a tremendous amount of weight. "I looked like a skeleton," Bruno said. He could hardly walk. He failed a physical that would have enabled him to come to the United States. The Sammartinos had to wait for another chance to enter the States.

Finally, in 1950, the family boarded a boat for the United States. When they arrived in Pittsburgh, Bruno met his father for the first time. He was fifteen years old. Bruno had heard that the streets of the United States were paved with gold, but he wasn't impressed when he first saw Pittsburgh, his new home. Pizzoferrato might have been small and poverty-stricken, but it was picturesque. Pittsburgh, a city in which steel was the major industry, was dirty and smoky.

There were other problems. In Pizzoferrato, everybody was Italian. In Pittsburgh, the Sammartinos were one of the first Italian families on the block. He felt like an outsider. "When I came to this country, I was your real eighty-pound weakling," Bruno told *People* magazine. "We were one of the first Italian families on the block and my brother [Paul] and I got the heck beat out of us because we couldn't speak English."

Bruno and Paul wanted to join the Young Mens' Hebrew Association (YMHA) so they could use exer-cise equipment and build up muscles. Unfortunately, that was easier said than done. The YMHA had a membership fee of

Bruno (right) with his brother, Paul, and his sister, Mary

thirteen dollars per person. That was a lot of money for two poor immigrant kids from Italy. Bruno and Paul went to a nearby town where rich people lived, knocked on doors, and offered to mow their lawns. Before long, they had earned the membership money.

Bruno spent most of his time learn-ing English and working out with weights. He attended Schenley High School in Pittsburgh and joined the football team.

Bruno became huge. He played on the offensive and defensive lines. In his spare time, he watched pro wrestling on a neighbor's television (his family couldn't afford one). He quickly became an outstanding wrestler and made the high school varsity team weighing 225 pounds. "All through high school, I wrestled whenever I could," Bruno recalled. "It was hard to find competition. I beat everybody."

One day, Bruno's gym teacher saw him challenging other kids to wrestling matches. "If you like wrestling so much, I have a friend who's a coach at Pitt," the gym teacher said. "How would you like to go over there?"

Pitt was the University of Pittsburgh, which had an outstanding wrestling team, coached by Rex Perry. Of course, Bruno was eager to work with Perry and wrestle with the college kids. Bruno started visiting Perry after school and training with the team. He became bigger and stronger because of his bodybuilding. He wrestled five days a week and worked out with weights after each session.

In 1955, Bruno appeared on a local television station, KDKA, and demonstrated weightlifting. In 1956, he narrowly lost out to Paul Anderson for a spot on the United States Olympic weightlifting team. Anderson weighed 365 pounds! Losing to a much bigger man was certainly no embarrassment.

After graduating from high school, Bruno worked briefly as an apprentice carpenter. He also met his future wife, Carol. She was the sister of his training partner. Bruno joined the air force and was stationed at a base in Lackland, Texas. While he served in the air force, Bruno continued to compete as a wrestler and weightlifter in matches against men from other air force bases.

Everything was going well in Bruno's life. When he left the air force, he hoped to find a good job. He had met the woman he wanted to marry. He was no longer a weakling, and he was becoming well known because of his TV appearances. Life was good for Bruno. It was about to get better.

# A Rough Start

Although Bruno Sammartino went on to achieve fame and fortune as a wrestler, the sport he was best at in the late 1950s was weightlifting. In 1958, Bruno won the North American power lifting contest in Oklahoma City, Oklahoma. When he returned to Pittsburgh, the television station that carried wrestling invited him to appear on its sports show.

Bruno appeared on TV with his trophy and was interviewed about his plans."I said I wanted to go to the Olympic Games," Bruno recalled. "Rudy Miller, who was involved in wrestling for many years, was watching the show in the studio, since wrestling was on next. After I finished the show, he approached me and said, 'I was listening to your interview. You said you've been wrestling a long time. I'm a promoter. Have you thought about turning pro?'"

Bruno, who was making a good living working as an apprentice carpenter, told Miller he'd think about it. But in 1959, Bruno married Carol. She didn't want him to become a pro wrestler, but Miller was persistent. In December 1959, Sammartino decided he wanted to wrestle professionally.

Miller brought Bruno to New York for a tryout. Toots Mondt, a powerful promoter, checked out Bruno. He and Vince McMahon Sr., another top promoter, decided to have Bruno sign a contract. The contract was for $250 a week. To Bruno, that sounded like a lot of money. "I was naive," he said. "I found out I had to pay for all my own plane fares and hotel rooms."

In his first pro match on December 17, 1959, in Pittsburgh, Bruno beat Dmitri Grabowski in nineteen seconds. Thanks to his amateur skills, size, and power, he would win 192 of his first 193 matches. Bruno was 6 feet tall and weighed 265 pounds. He was billed as the World's Strongest Man. That wasn't just hype. In 1959, he had set a world

*Bruno Sammartino*

record in the bench press, lifting 565 pounds. The record went unbeaten for nine years.

But things did not always go well for Bruno. He was a stranger in the sport. "The first three years were a little rough because I came into a world that was awfully

Sammartino beat Mighty Zuma at Madison Square Garden in 1959.

strange to me and I was always sort of a naive guy," Bruno said. "I believed easily in people and so I had people direct me in the wrong ways. The competition was okay, but the worst part was trying to get your name established, trying to do something so people would know you and the promoters would give you a break." By no means, however, was Bruno being ignored. In 1960, he teamed with Antonio "Argentina" Rocca, who along with Buddy Rogers was one of the top stars of the era.

The most memorable match during Bruno's first few years as a pro wrestler occurred in April 1960, when he wrestled Haystacks Calhoun. If Bruno was big, Calhoun was gigantic. By some estimates, he weighed over 600 pounds. Calhoun, like Bruno, was a fan favorite, and when the two met for the first time at Madison Square Garden in New York, the fans didn't know who to root for.

Bruno knew he was in for the toughest test of his young wrestling career. When Calhoun caught him in a headlock late in the match, Bruno had to think quickly. He reached around, grabbed Calhoun's gigantic legs, and slammed him to the mat. The crowd couldn't believe what it had seen. Bruno was the first wrestler to slam Calhoun! "When I picked him up, I thought the roof on the Garden was going to go off," Bruno recalled. "When I dropped him the whole ring nearly caved in. But after that, people could remember my name."

The fans loved him. Unlike Buddy Rogers, who was a showman and liked to taunt his opponents and the fans, Bruno was an honest, no-nonsense wrestler. He didn't care about putting on a show. He cared about wrestling and winning. He rarely broke the rules. And due to his working-class background, the fans in New York loved him. He was a regular guy.

Calhoun and Sammartino had several more exciting matches, most of which ended in draws. Bruno bodyslammed Calhoun again in Chicago. One time, Haystacks flipped Bruno to the mat. "He was the first man I met who was as strong as me," Bruno said.

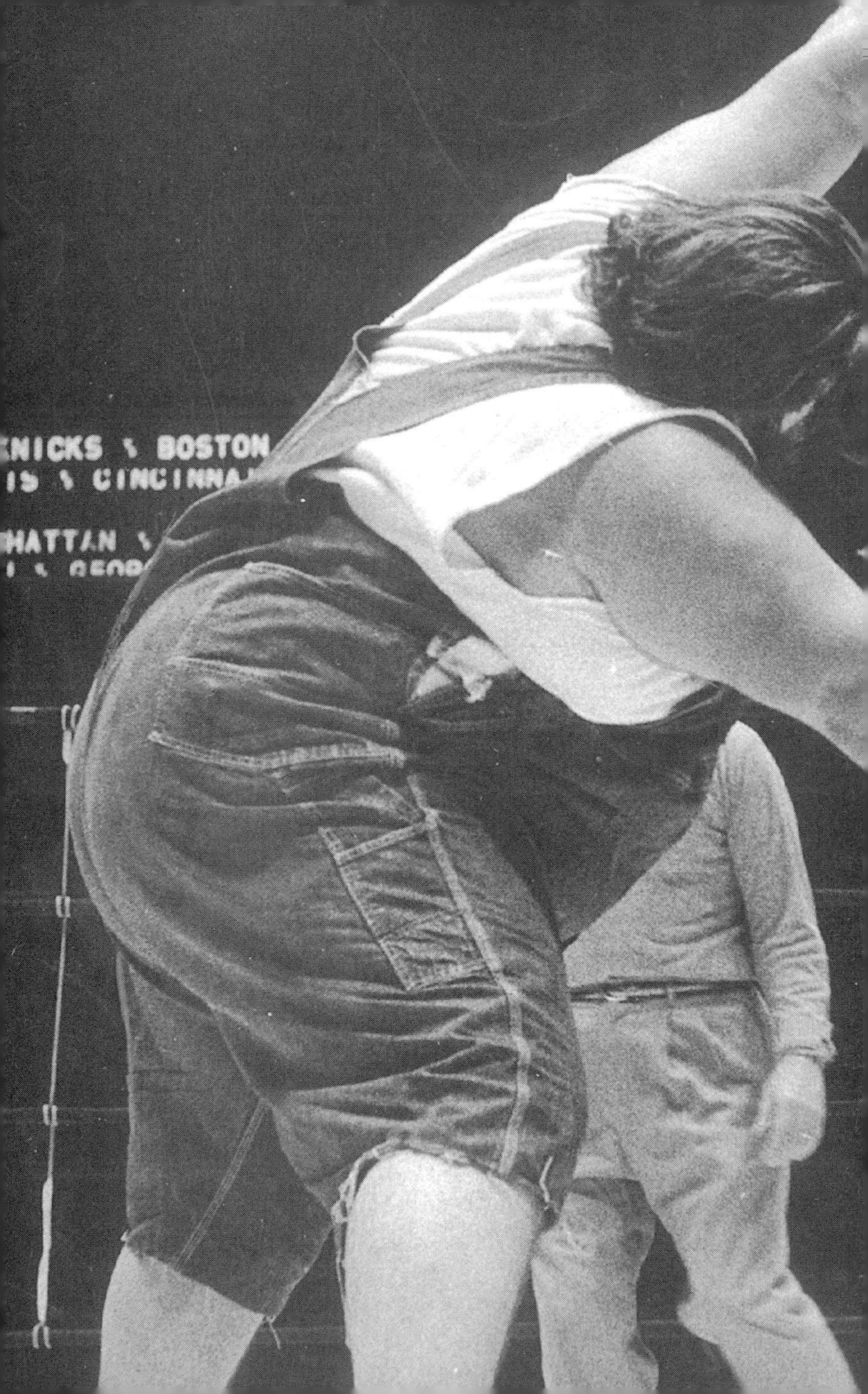
NICKS BOSTON

Sammartino grappling with Haystacks Calhoun at Madison Square Garden in New York in 1961.

Bruno showed his strength in the matches against Calhoun. He proved his wrestling ability in a match against Rocca. With over eighteen minutes gone in this close match, Bruno stunned Rocca with a series of shoulder blocks. Bruno attacked Rocca in the corner. The referee told him to break it up, but Bruno didn't obey quickly enough. He lost by disqualification.

Meanwhile, Bruno was getting frustrated. The promoters were refusing to grant him a match against new National Wrestling Alliance (NWA) world champion, Buddy Rogers. The NWA was the most powerful wrestling organization in the world. Its champion was considered the best wrestler in the world.

Bruno was certain he could beat Rogers, if only he was given the chance. "I felt I deserved a shot at the title and Rogers wouldn't even recognize me as a challenger," Bruno said. "I had made my intentions known to promoter Vince McMahon Sr. He told me to relax and not do anything rash."

Bruno didn't listen to that advice. When his contract expired in 1962, he decided to wrestle in Canada. On May 11, 1962, Sammartino and Whipper Billy Watson combined to win the international tag team title in Toronto. He pinned Killer Kowalski for the Canadian heavyweight title. Before long, Bruno was making $2,000 a week, far more than he had been making

Bruno knocks down Buddy Rogers, a showman who liked to taunt his opponents and the fans.

in the United States. He fought some matches against Rogers, too.

Rogers beat Bruno by countout in their first meeting. Their second match took place on August 2, 1962 at Maple Leaf Gardens in Toronto. During the match, Bruno rebounded off the ropes and struck Rogers in the groin. Rogers fell to the mat holding his lower abdomen. Referee Tiger Tasker counted to ten. Rogers had been counted out. Bruno was the NWA's new world champion, or so it seemed.

Bruno, as it turned out, was a bigger sportsman than anybody realized. When Tasker tried to lift his arm, Bruno refused to budge. Bruno then grabbed the ring microphone and, in Italian, told the fans he didn't think the championship should change hands because one man was unable to continue. "I know I can beat Rogers," Bruno declared. "I'll do it the right way or not at all."

The belt was returned to Rogers, who had to be carried back to the locker room. Bruno spent eighteen months in Canada. During this time, he won his first important heavyweight title and proved he could beat the NWA world champion. Promoter Vince McMahon Sr. finally realized he was better off with Bruno than without him. He phoned Bruno and tried to lure him back to the United States by offering anything Bruno wanted. What Bruno wanted most, of course, was another shot at Rogers.

# 3 The Heavyweight Champion of the World

The wrestling world was changing in 1963. On January 24, 1963, Buddy Rogers lost the NWA world heavyweight title to Lou Thesz. The outcome was controversial. In those days, most championship matches were determined by the best two of three falls. This match was only one fall. At the time, several promoters in the Northeast, including Vince McMahon Sr., disagreed with the other NWA promoters over how to do business. Because the match was only one fall, not two of three falls, the Northeast promoters refused to recognize Thesz as world champion.

The Northeast promoters resolved the problem by breaking away from the NWA and forming the World Wide Wrestling Federation (WWWF). In April 1963 in Rio de Janeiro, Brazil, Rogers won a tournament and became the first WWWF world champion. Almost immediately, promoters signed Rogers for a title defense against Bruno on May 17, 1963 at Madison Square Garden. "As far as ambition, I figured this would be the match that would make me if I beat Rogers," Bruno said. "I thought, 'Wow, this might be the turning point in my life.'"

Bruno didn't know that Rogers had suffered a mild heart attack a month earlier and wasn't in top physical form. If he had known, he might not have been quite so nervous before the match. He paced up and down the dressing room for two hours. A cold sweat covered his body. But Bruno was more than ready for Rogers. With only thirty seconds gone in the match, Bruno lifted Rogers above his head in a move called the backbreaker. Rogers screamed out in pain. Bruno dropped him to the mat and covered him for the pin. The match lasted only forty-seven seconds. The crowd was ecstatic. The beloved working-class boy had vanquished the hated Rogers.

At age twenty-six, Bruno was the new WWWF world champion. He could hardly believe his good fortune. "I remember I was walking back to the hotel after the match and I was numb," Bruno recalled. "I felt great but I felt scared. Will this new life work? I wondered. I had a lot of worries on my mind. For a few split seconds after the match, I was the happiest guy in the world. All of a sudden, there were so many uncertainties ahead of me. I wondered if people would come to see me as a featured star."

When he got back to his hotel room, Bruno received a phone call from his sister Mary. "My God, Bruno!" she exclaimed. "They just said on the eleven o'clock news that you won the title at Madison Square Garden." Suddenly, Bruno felt great. But the victory was not only big for Bruno, it was big for the WWWF, too. The brand-new federation needed a popular star to give it credibility.

Bruno turned out to be just the man the WWWF needed. "Judging from the enormous reaction that night, I knew my future was bright," Bruno told *Inside Wrestling* magazine years later. "I was young and that victory gave me confidence. Wrestling hadn't been doing too well in New York at the time, but selling out the Garden became the norm after that match." The victory turned Bruno into a superstar. The eighty-pound weakling had become the heavyweight champion of the world.

# Monsoon and Blassie

News about Bruno Sammartino's amazing victory spread quickly around the wrestling world. The rematch between Bruno and Rogers was scheduled for October 4, 1963. The fans' demand for tickets became so great, however, that the match had to be moved to an outdoor baseball stadium in New Jersey. The rematch never happened, though, because Rogers hadn't fully recovered from his heart attack.

Meanwhile, Bruno was busy with a new rival: Gorilla Monsoon, another huge wrestler who weighed over 350 pounds. Bruno and Bobo Brazil battled to a draw with Monsoon and Hans Mortier on September 16, 1963. Monsoon, a hated villain with sadistic tendencies, had his eye on Bruno's newly won title.

When Rogers backed out of the match against Bruno, a tournament was held to pick a new number-one contender for the world title. Monsoon won the tournament and would face Bruno on October 4, 1963. "There's no way I'm going to lose," Monsoon said. "There's nobody in the WWWF that can beat me, and that includes Sammartino. Nobody's beaten me before, and they're not going to start now. I've proven that I'm unbeatable."

Over 18,000 fans attended the Sammartino vs. Monsoon match. Bruno and Monsoon could barely budge each other. As the match continued, blood poured down the faces of both men. They were exhausted. Eighteen minutes into the match, Monsoon made a critical mistake: He threw Bruno over the top rope, an illegal move. The referee immediately disqualified Monsoon.

A crowd of 18,969 attended the rematch at Madison Square Garden. Bruno and Monsoon wrestled all out. Monsoon, who weighed in at 367 pounds, dominated early on. Bruno rallied and weakened

Monsoon with a wristlock. Desperate to escape, Monsoon eventually spun out of the move. They took turns slamming each other to the mat. Bruno then whipped Monsoon into the ropes, but Monsoon avoided Bruno's clothesline on the rebound. Bruno again whipped Monsoon into the ropes. This time, the two big men collided into each other. They fell to the mat. The referee began to count. Twenty-one minutes and eleven seconds into the match, the referee had counted to ten. Both men were still lying on the mat. The match was ruled a double countout.

Bruno pinned Monsoon in their next match but this feud had only just begun. Bruno and Monsoon wrestled all over the wrestling circuit—in Philadelphia, Pittsburgh, and Washington, DC. Sellout crowds greeted them wherever they went. Monsoon gave Bruno some of the toughest tests of his life, but Bruno was determined to retain his title. This would become a trademark of Bruno's title reign: He often came close to losing against outstanding opponents, but they never pinned him.

Bruno and Monsoon had their most memorable match on May 11, 1964, at Madison Square Garden. The match lasted one hour and ten minutes. Bruno and Monsoon exchanged the advantage several times during the match. There were several near pins. At one point, both men were flat on their backs until the eight count. The match ended in a draw at the eleven o'clock curfew. Monsoon cracked a couple of ribs and hurt his knee during the match. Bruno's entire body ached.

Now that Bruno was on top of the wrestling world, every big-time wrestler wanted a shot at him. One of the top rulebreakers of the time was Fred Blassie, a bloodthirsty brawler who had no respect for scientific wrestling. Bruno wrestled Blassie for the first time in the summer of 1964 at an outdoor baseball stadium in Jersey City, New Jersey. "I knew a great deal about him," Bruno told *Wrestling World* magazine. "I knew that he was a veteran who had been around a long time and knew every trick in the book."

Blassie was wily and cunning, indeed. He used moves Bruno had never seen before. The match groaned on for over an hour. It was a hot night and both men were exhausted. After over an hour, Blassie misfired with a drop kick and struck the referee, who fell out of the ring. Bruno covered Blassie for the pin, but the ref was unconscious. When Bruno tried to help the ref, Blassie attacked him from behind and kicked him in the groin.

Bruno collapsed to the mat in unbearable pain. The referee climbed back into the ring and counted out Bruno, who couldn't get up. Blassie was the winner. "The fans were outraged by Blassie's illegal shot," Bruno recalled in his autobiography.

Within seconds, chairs started flying into the ring, all aimed at Blassie's head. Then the crowd pressed around the ring and started shaking the posts, whipping the ropes back and forth wildly. Blassie stood in the center of the ring, clenching his fists and shouting that he was ready to take on anybody.

The police charged in and attempted to break up the melee with no immediate success. They called for reinforcements and even requested that some of the other wrestlers help get Blassie out of danger. But no matter what the police tried, the fans held Blassie hostage. Chairs rained in from every direction and Bruno remembered hugging the mat, trying to keep from being hit. Eventually, police and wrestlers formed a human circle around Blassie and escorted him out of the park.

Blassie didn't get the championship belt because he hadn't pinned Bruno. Bruno felt terrible for days after the match. He knew, deep down in his heart, that he had pinned Blassie while the referee was down. "It was just one of those things that the referee missed," Bruno said. "He didn't see me pin Blassie because he was out of the ring."

Blassie beat Bruno one more time by countout, but Bruno got revenge on August 21, 1964 at Madison Square Garden. Bruno caught Blassie in a bear hug, then scored the pin. Having passed another test, Bruno was truly becoming a living legend.

# Lining 'Em Up and Knocking 'Em Down 5

In the following years, the greatest wrestlers in the world would line up for shots at Bruno and his championship belt. The list reads like a who's who of wrestling in the 60s and 70s: Killer Kowalski, Ivan Koloff, Gorilla Monsoon, Waldo von Erich, Haystacks Calhoun, Gene Kiniski, Bill Miller, Ernie Ladd, Bobo Brazil, Hans Mortier, Professor Tanaka, Ray Stevens, Johnny Valentine,

Bill Watts, and Blackjack Mulligan. None of them could beat Bruno for the belt.

Gene Kiniski was a future NWA world champion who

thought he had what it took to beat Bruno. He almost did. On November 17, 1964, at Madison Square Garden, Kiniski covered Bruno for the pin. Bruno smartly draped a leg over the lower rope. The referee made the three count, then realized what Bruno had done. He ordered Kiniski to break the hold. Bruno was declared the winner.

Bruno kept defending his title. His schedule was hectic. He wrestled seventy-four matches during the first four months of 1965. In some of those matches, he teamed with Bill Watts or Haystacks Calhoun, who had become his friend.

Bruno was popular wherever he went. His once-a-month matches at Madison Square Garden never failed to draw sellout crowds. Bruno's inside-the-ring feuds usually followed a pattern. A wrestler would challenge him. In their first two or three matches, Bruno would win or lose by disqualification or countout. He often needed time to figure out and frustrate his opponents. By the fourth or fifth meeting, however, Bruno became the dominant wrestler.

Gorilla Monsoon, however, refused to go away. Their feud raged into 1967. On February 27, another sellout crowd at Madison Square Garden watched Monsoon beat Bruno by countout. A month later at the Garden, Bruno and Monsoon had been battling for ninety minutes when the eleven o'clock curfew approached. With the seconds ticking off and the match about to end, Bruno covered Monsoon for the pin. The referee counted to two, then stopped counting when the curfew bell rang. The match was declared a draw.

A few months later, Bruno beat Monsoon in a Texas Death Match. In a spectacular six-man tag-team match—three men on each team—Monsoon smashed Bruno over the head with a chair. Bruno was carried away on a stretcher. Minutes later, Bruno ran back to the ring with his bloody head bandaged. The crowd went wild as Bruno stormed into the ring and slammed Monsoon for the decisive pin. "He'll never beat me," Bruno declared. "He doesn't have what it takes to beat me."

The feud finally ended in a way no one could have anticipated. In 1969, Bruno defended his world title on TV. This was a rare television appearance. The reason Bruno hardly ever wrestled on TV was because promoters wanted to save him for arena matches. The promoters wanted fans to pay to watch him.

That night, Monsoon was standing in the arena runway watching Bruno's match. As Bruno was attacked by two rulebreakers, Monsoon walked to the ring. The fans were sure he was going to attack Bruno. But he didn't. He helped him. "I don't know why he did it, but I'm glad he did," Bruno said. "I guess I owe him one."

Bruno returned the favor. A few weeks later, Monsoon was wrestling when he got doubleteamed by two rulebreakers. This time, Bruno ran into the ring and saved Monsoon. A feud that had lasted six years and hundreds of matches ended with a handshake. Of course, Monsoon was only one of hundreds of wrestlers who wanted a piece of Bruno. Having Monsoon out of the way didn't mean there weren't plenty of other challengers for Bruno to worry about.

# **6** The Russian Bear

Nobody knew what it was like to be Bruno Sammartino. That's because nobody had ever remained the champion for so long. He was a hero everywhere he went. In Japan, he successfully defended the WWWF title against Shohei "Giant" Baba, one of the best Japanese wrestlers of all time. Whether in Japan or the United States, Bruno never had an easy match. "My whole life has been tough and everything I've accomplished has been from hard work," Bruno said. "That's the way I want to be recognized. I pride myself on my reputation. I never drink in public. I have never been high in my life. I won't do beer commercials. It wouldn't be the Bruno that all my people know."

His people loved him, but they had no idea what he had sacrificed to become the Living Legend. He hardly ever saw his wife and three children back home. The travel was constant. Vacations were rare. Before some matches, his body was so wracked with pain that he would have loved to take the night off. "When you

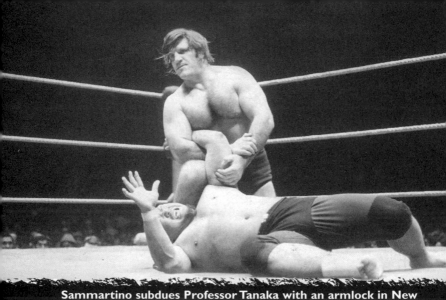

Sammartino subdues Professor Tanaka with an armlock in New York City in January 1973.

have the belt, you can't take it off," Bruno insisted. "You're a slave to that thing. If it was up to the promoters, I'd be fighting one day in Chicago, the next day in Tokyo, twice a day, seven days a week."

By 1970, Bruno had been champion for seven years. His back was wearing down. He was in almost constant pain. Of course, his opponents didn't know or care about that. Most people considered Bruno unbeatable. After all, he hadn't been pinned cleanly in seven years. That's why few people gave Ivan Koloff, known as the Russian Bear, much chance against Bruno. Their first match on April 4, 1970, at Boston Garden ended in a draw when the referee was accidentally knocked unconscious.

Everybody figured the same old pattern would continue: They'd wrestle to a few draws, then finally Bruno would get the best of his Russian foe. "I don't pay much attention to odds," Koloff said. "All I want to do is get that Sammartino in the ring and take the title away from him. I had him last time, but it was halted. It won't happen next time. I guarantee it.

Bruno won't have time to think. I'll destroy him."

Koloff was an unusual wrestler. The fans hated him and he frequently resorted to rulebreaking tactics. But although he stood 5 feet 10 inches and weighed 300 pounds, he had tremendous speed and fantastic moves. He was a scientific rule-breaker. "There was a lot of action in our matches, especially our first cage match in Madison Square Garden," Bruno said. "Fans were responsive because Koloff was so rugged-looking and vicious."

Three days before a rematch against Koloff at Madison Square Garden, Bruno wrestled ruthless villain George "The Animal" Steele. During the match, Steele smashed an aluminum chair over Bruno's back. Although he was hurt, Bruno won the match. The injury, however, had a lasting effect. As match time approached on January 18, 1971, Bruno seriously considered calling off his bout against Koloff. "I could have called the match off, but I didn't want to disappoint my fans," Bruno said. "I had already beaten Koloff four or five times and if I wasn't in such pain, I would have done it again."

The match went on. Bruno whipped Koloff into a corner and charged after him. Koloff responded with a vicious kick to Bruno's midsection. Bruno went down. Koloff mounted the turnbuckle and prepared to deliver his

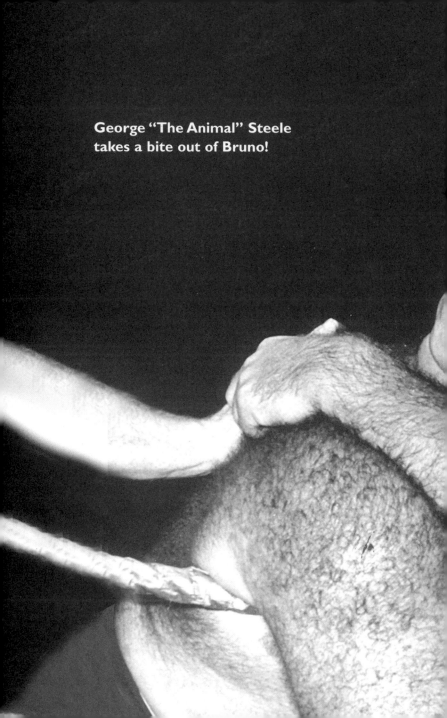

George "The Animal" Steele
takes a bite out of Bruno!

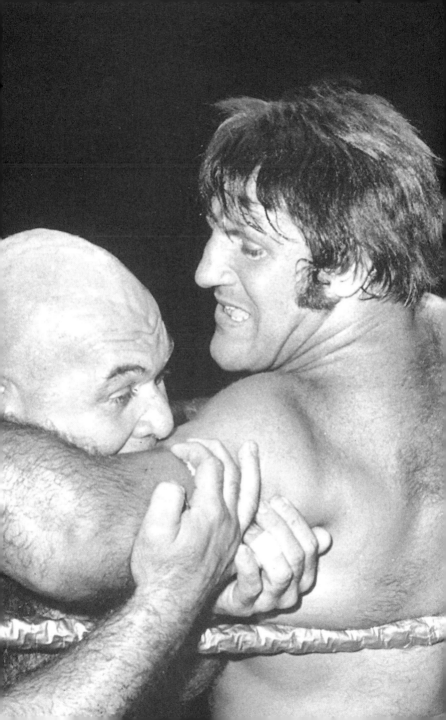

atomic knee drop. Bruno couldn't move. Koloff landed the knee drop perfectly across Bruno's shoulders and covered him for the pin.

The crowd watched in disbelief: After seven years, eight months, and one day, Bruno had finally lost the WWWF world title. The crowd was silent as Bruno walked back to the dressing room. For a minute, he thought he had gone deaf. Then a fan screamed, "Bruno, we love you!"

"That really hurt me," Bruno said. "I went to that dressing room and I was depressed. Losing the belt really didn't make me so sad. It was the people's reaction that did. They really cared for me. That touched me."

Bruno later revealed that he had separated his shoulder in the match against Steele. He had been wrestling with one arm. "I had been wrestling for a couple of years in real agony," he revealed. "I had some serious back problems. I also had a very bad shoulder and collarbone. Well, when you're in pain constantly, you lose the value of things. The title wasn't so important to me anymore. It was getting real hard to train, no less wrestle. In fact, sometimes when I wrestled, my legs would actually go numb due to disc and vertebrae troubles. It was a horrible experience."

When Bruno thought about all this, he decided it was a blessing to lose the title. Now he could spend more time with his wife and children and allow his injuries to heal. "I was thirty-four years old and I hadn't seen my ten-year-old son grow up," Bruno said. "I wanted to be more of a father to my three-year-old twins. When I lost the title, I decided to spend more time with my family and friends."

Bruno's friends included some famous people, such as comedian Jimmy Durante and opera star Franco Corelli. Bruno was a big opera fan. He often attended the opera in Philadelphia and New York. He once told *Sports Illustrated* that if he had the choice between being a wrestler or an opera star, he would have become an opera star.

Bruno cut down his schedule. He underwent physical therapy at a hospital in Pennsylvania. The thought of retiring kept crossing his mind. Bruno healed his injuries as much as they could be healed. He resumed weightlifting and running. He spent quality time with his wife and children. After a year of this, he decided it wasn't quite time to retire. "I got calls from promoters all over the country," Bruno said. "I told them I wasn't going to overdo it, but I'd take a match here and there. I wrestled in St. Louis, Missouri, California, and other areas." Wrestling wasn't ready to say good-bye to the Living Legend. And the Living Legend wasn't ready to say good-bye to the life of a world champion.

# 7 A Champion Again

Los Angeles was buzzing with excitement. For the first time in a year, Bruno Sammartino was returning to wrestling. He was going to wrestle in a twenty-two-man battle royal. A battle royal is a free-for-all in which the object is to eliminate your opponents by dumping them over the top rope. The last man standing is the winner. This type of match had been outlawed in most parts of the country.

On January 14, 1972, a sellout crowd of 11,772 packed Olympic Auditorium to watch Bruno wrestle in his first battle royal. All of the years as champion hadn't given him time for such gimmick matches. "At first I was a little confused, what with twenty-two wrestlers and all," Bruno said. "I was worried about people charging up on me from behind and things like that. But I decided I'd take care of one guy at a time and let the chips falls where they may. You can't plan strategy for a match like this. Everything's kind of freelance. It seemed I was in there for a long time, so I figured I must have been doing something right." Bruno won the battle royal, much to the crowd's delight, and the prize of $11,000.

A lot had changed since Bruno lost the WWWF belt. In February 1971, fan favorite Pedro Morales beat Ivan Koloff for the title. Bruno knew Morales well and was delighted that his friend, a fan favorite, was champion. During the summer of 1972, Bruno and Morales joined forces for a televised tag-team match against Professor Tanaka and Mr. Fuji, the WWWF world tag-team champions.

Tanaka and Fuji were well known for their devious behavior. During the match, Morales mistakenly leaped onto Bruno when Fuji moved out of the way. Later, Fuji threw a handful of salt into Bruno's eyes. Blinded, Bruno began swinging wildly. Morales rushed in to help, but was accidentally struck by Bruno. Morales fell to the mat and Tanaka threw salt in his eyes. Tanaka then grabbed Bruno and threw him on top of Morales. Now both men were blinded. Thinking they were wrestling with their opponents, Bruno and Morales started punching each other. The referee ended the match.

Suddenly, Morales and Bruno were at odds. Each man blamed the other for what happened. Promoters, sensing the opportunity for a sensational match, immediately signed Morales and Bruno up for a title bout at Shea Stadium in New York. "I had to take this match to prove I was a worthy champion, even though I didn't want the pressure again," Bruno said.

**Bruno Sammartino gets ready to slam Pedro Morales at Shea Stadium in New York in September 1972.**

On a cold, wet night, September 30, 1972, over 22,000 fans shivered in their seats at Shea Stadium to watch these two former friends. It was billed as the Wrestling Match of the Century. The first shock of the evening came when Bruno walked into the ring and was booed for the first time in his career.

Many experts have offered their opinions as to why Bruno was booed that night. Morales was a fan favorite. Perhaps fans didn't think it was right for Bruno to challenge another fan favorite. Also, the fans who attended the monthly cards at Madison Square Garden were angry that Bruno was no longer appearing on a regular basis. Morales had replaced him in their hearts.

The match started at 9:45 PM, seventy-five minutes before the eleven o'clock curfew time in New York. Bruno, despite getting booed, wrestled cleanly. So did Morales. At one point, Bruno caught Morales in a backbreaker and Morales appeared to be on the verge of collapsing. Several times, both men laid dazed on the canvas. There were several near pins. After seventy-five minutes of sensational scientific action, the curfew bell rang. The match was declared a draw.

The crowd was angry. It wanted to see a conclusion to the match. Several fans jumped onto the baseball dugouts and shook their fists at the wrestlers. But then Bruno and Morales smiled at each other and raised a pair of American flags. They hugged. The fans cheered. The next month, Morales and Sammartino were back together as tag-team partners.

Bruno wrestled infrequently over the next year. Morales turned out to be a worthy champion. But on December 1, 1973, Morales lost the world title to Stan Stasiak. A few days later, Bruno received a call from Vince McMahon Sr. The number of wrestling fans at matches was down in New York. A rulebreaker was champion. The WWWF needed Bruno. "He called a number of times and said 'Bruno you have to come back. Things are slipping away. All I ask is one year,' " Bruno recalled. "He told me if I came back he would just use me in the big shows, so I went back."

Madison Square Garden was packed to the rafters once again when Bruno faced Stasiak for the world title on December 10, 1973. In a spectacular performance, Bruno pinned Stasiak to win his second WWWF world title. Less than two years after he had considered retiring, Bruno was back on top of the world.

# 8 Farewell to the Living Legend

He was a thirty-seven-year-old, two-time champion with a bad back and a family who needed him. He had considered retirement and allowed himself to be talked out of it. In 1963, Bruno Sammartino had single-handedly saved the WWWF. In the mid-1970s, against all odds, he did it again.

In many ways, Bruno's second world title reign was more spectacular than his first. Because he was older, he had to rely on determination and intelligence to win his matches. His opponents were often much younger and much bigger than him. He defeated 315-pound Don Leo Jonathan. He overcame Russian madman Nikolai Volkoff. He turned back challenges from Bobby Duncum and Olympic weightlifter Ken Patera, and feuded once again with Ivan Koloff.

The fans were even more support-ive than before. Madison Square Garden, which held 21,000 fans for wrestling, wasn't big enough for Bruno: The people who ran the Garden had to open the the-ater next door so fans could watch his matches on closed-circuit TV. On March

Bruno enters
a steel cage
match.

17, 1975, more than 26,000 fans packed the Garden to watch a Texas Death Match between Bruno and Spiros Arion (managed by Fred Blassie). After nearly twenty minutes of grueling action, Bruno slammed Arion to the canvas and scored the pin.

Bruno's second title reign went on and on. One year. Then two. Then a third year. In 1976, he faced the most serious threat of his career. In a match on May 1, 1976, at Madison Square Garden, tough guy Stan Hansen threw Bruno from the ring. After the match, Bruno was diagnosed with a broken neck. "Yours is a very serious injury," the doctor told him. "I don't know if you are interested in returning to the ring, but I'm not going to rule it out for you."

Bruno was in traction for five weeks. As he lay in bed and thought about Hansen, the desire for revenge grew stronger. Doctors finally gave Bruno clearance to wrestle. On June 15, 1976, at Shea Stadium, Hansen and Bruno went head-to-head one more time. Hansen never stood a chance. Wrestling with a fury no one had ever seen, Bruno exacted revenge by crushing Hansen.

Bruno, however, had been lucky. The injury he suffered against Hansen could have been crippling. Earlier that year, he got a big break in a match against "Superstar" Billy Graham, a

6-foot 5-inch, 285-pound Californian. Graham dominated the match and won when the referee mistakenly counted out Bruno after ten seconds instead of the required twenty. If the match had continued, Bruno might have been pinned. Because he lost by countout, Bruno retained the title.

Graham once again wrapped his big paws around Bruno on April 30, 1977 in Baltimore, Maryland. After twenty minutes, Graham whipped Bruno off the ropes and caught him in his Superstar Bear Hug. Graham slammed Bruno to the mat. Then, with his feet on the ropes for leverage, he scored the pin. Bruno's second title reign was over.

Bruno failed several times to regain the title from Graham. Several matches were fought to draws. Sammartino vs. Graham was by far the hottest feud of 1977. Despite the loss to Graham, Bruno's legend had grown bigger than ever. He was the first wrestler to appear on the TV show *Greatest Sports Legends*. Profiles about Bruno appeared in the magazines *Sports Illustrated, Sport,* and *People*. The world title slipped further out of reach, changing hands from Graham to fan favorite Bob Backlund. Bruno's popularity soared nonetheless.

Bruno had one more big battle left in him. Several years earlier in Pittsburgh,

Bruno had befriended a young high school wrestler named Larry Zbyszko. After attending college, Zbyszko became Bruno's protégé. The teacher taught the youngster everything he knew about wrestling. Zbyszko was a clean-cut kid who wanted to follow in the master's footsteps.

In 1980, shortly after turning pro, Zbyszko convinced Bruno to wrestle him in an exhibition match. Bruno was reluctant, but finally agreed. In early March, the two had their exhibition match. Bruno dominated and, after several minutes, suggested to Zbyszko that they stop. "Larry, enough's enough," Bruno said as he opened the ropes for Zbyszko. "Let's call it a night."

Before Bruno knew what happened, Zbyszko drove a knee into his midsection. Bruno dropped to his knees in pain. Then Zbyszko grabbed a chair and slammed Bruno over the head. Bruno had to be taken to a nearby hospital for stitches. The feud was on.

On March 24, 1980, the largest crowd to ever watch a sporting event at Madison Square Garden saw Bruno's vicious side. He was disqualified because he wouldn't break an illegal hold he had on Larry Zbyszko. On August 9, 1980, a crowd of 46,000 at Shea Stadium watched Bruno beat Zbyszko in a cage match. As always, Bruno had exacted revenge.

In late 1981, Bruno announced that he would retire after wrestling George "The Animal" Steele at the Meadowlands arena in New Jersey. After beating Steele in less than fifteen minutes in front of a sell-out crowd, Bruno grabbed the ring microphone and thanked the fans for their support. He then went on a two-week farewell tour of Japan. Bruno didn't walk quietly into the sunset, however. In 1982, his son David, wrestling as Bruno Sammartino Jr., made his professional debut. Bruno enjoyed teaming up with his son several times. After all, they had spent so little time together while David was growing up. His son's wrestling ability did not rival Bruno's, but then again, nobody's did.

Sammartino jogs in his hometown of Pittsburgh in 1983, after he officially retired.

If one were to divide the second half of the twentieth century into wrestling eras, there would be the Bruno Sammartino era from 1963 to 1980, and the Hulk Hogan era from 1984 to the present. One era couldn't have been more different than the other. The Bruno Sammartino era was about hard work and clean wrestling, without glitz or

Sammartino, now in his sixties, holds up a drawing from his championship days.

glamour. The Hulk Hogan era is about rock 'n' wrestling, celebrities, and show-time. As one era ended and another began, Bruno began to resent what was happening to the sport he adored. He thought it had become a circus. To this day, Bruno refuses to admit that in 1987, he actually teamed with Hogan for a match in Baltimore.

There's no doubt that if Bruno was in his prime today, he'd be a millionaire, just like Hogan, The Rock, and Ric Flair. But Bruno has no regrets. Today, living in Pittsburgh with his wife Carol, he is saddened by what wrestling has become. But he can take solace in the fact that there has been only one Bruno Sammartino, only one Living Legend.

# Glossary

**armlock**  A move in which an opponent's arm is held bent behind his or her back.

**atomic knee drop**  Offensive move in which the attacker stands behind the opponent, grabs him or her around the midsection with one arm, and hooks one of the opponent's legs with the other arm. The opponent is then lifted and dropped, tailbone-first, onto the attacker's knee.

**backbreaker**  A submission move in which the wrestler lifts the opponent over his or her head by gripping the opponent's back.

**card**  List of matches in a wrestling show.

**clothesline**  An offensive move in which the attacking wrestler sticks out his or her arm and uses it to strike the victim in the neck. The clothesline is often executed by whipping the opponent into the ropes, then striking him or her in the neck on the rebound.

**counter attack/counter wrestling**  A defensive strategy in which the wrestler's goal is to break or wrestle his or her way out of the opponent's offensive move.

**countout**   A wrestler is counted out if he or she is out of the ring for twenty seconds or more. When the wrestler leaves the ring, the referee begins the count at one. If the wrestler is counted out, he or she is disqualified.

**curfew**   The prescribed time at which a wrestling card must end. Certain states, such as New York, have had eleven o'clock curfews for wrestling cards.

**disqualification**  In wrestling, a wrestler can lose by disqualification if he or she uses a foreign object, refuses to obey the referee's orders, breaks the rules repeatedly, is counted out of the ring, or if another person interferes on his or her behalf. Except in the event of a double disqualification, in which both wrestlers lose, the victory is awarded to the opponent. In most championship matches, the belt does not change hands on a disqualification, only on a pin or submission.

**feud**  A series of matches between two wrestlers or tag teams. Many times one wrestler will bad-mouth the other wrestler or will sneak-attack the wrestler.

**flying head scissors**   A sensational aerial move in which the wrestler leaps into the air, wraps his or her legs around the opponent's neck, and tugs him or her to the mat.

**foreign object**   An illegal object used in the ring, such as a chair or a pencil.

**gimmick**   The personality of a wrestler.

**manager**   The person responsible for overseeing a wrestler's inside-the-ring and outside-the-ring activities. Managers often take care of a wrestler's business affairs (such as signing contracts and arranging matches) and also assist with strategy.

**pin**   When either both shoulders or both shoulder blades are held in contact with the mat for three continuous seconds. A pin ends a match.

**pinfall**   A win achieved by a pin.

**promoter**   The person responsible for hiring and contracting the wrestlers for a card or federation. The promoter is also responsible for deciding the match-ups for a card.

**scientific match**   A match between two or more wrestlers, in which the combatants rely mostly on amateur wrestling moves, rather than kicking and punching.

**small package**   A counter wrestling move in which the wrestler being pinned grabs the opponent's legs or upper body, rolls him or her over, and places him or her into pinning position.

**submission hold**   A move that makes an opponent give up without being pinned.

# For More Information

## Magazines

*Pro Wrestling Illustrated, The Wrestler, Inside Wrestling, Wrestle America,* and *Wrestling Superstars*
London Publishing Co.
7002 West Butler Pike
Ambler, PA 19002

*WCW Magazine*
P.O. Box 420235

Palm Coast, FL 32142-0235
(800) WCW-MAGS (929-6247)

*WOW Magazine*
McMillen Communications
P.O. Box 500
Missouri City, TX 77459-9904
Fax: (281) 261-5999
Web site: http://www.wowmagazine.com

# Web Sites

Dory Funk's Web Site
http://www.dory-funk.com

Professional Wrestling Online Museum
http://www.wrestlingmuseum.com

Pro Wrestling Torch newsletter
http://www.pwtorch.com

World Championship Wrestling
http://www.wcw.com

World Wrestling Federation
http://www.wwf.com

# For Further Reading

Albano, Lou, Bert Randolph Sugar, and
Michael Benson. *The Complete
Idiot's Guide to Pro Wrestling*,
2nd ed. New York: Alpha Books, 2000.

Archer, Jeff. *Theater in a Squared
Circle*. New York: White-Boucke
Publishing, 1998.

Cohen, Dan. *Wrestling Renegades: An In-Depth Look at Today's Superstars of Pro Wrestling.* New York: Archway, 1999.

Farley, Cal. *Two Thousand Sons: The Story of Cal Farley's Boys Ranch.* Washington: Phoenix Publishing, 1987.

Hofstede, David. *Slammin': Wrestling's Greatest Heroes and Villains.* New York: ECW Press, 1999.

Mazer, Sharon. *Professional Wrestling: Sport and Spectacle.* Jackson, MS: University Press of Mississippi, 1998.

Myers, Robert and Adolph Caso. *The Professional Wrestling Trivia Book,* 2nd ed. Boston, MA: Branden Books, 1999.

## Works Cited

Berger, Ira and Sheldon Widelitz. "Golden Grappler." *Italian American Magazine*, March 1977, pp. 45–49.

"Bruno Sammartino Beat 21 Opponents All In One Night." *The Wrestler,* May 1972, pp. 32–37.

Jerome, James F. "Wrestling Champ Sammartino, A Big Man At The

Bank." *People*, July 1, 1974, pp. 19–21.

Kupferberg, Herbert. "The Rough (and Rich) Life of a Wrestling Champ." *Parade*, February 15, 1976, pp. 12–16.

Sammartino, Bruno. *Bruno Sammartino: An Autobiography of Wrestling's Living Legend.* Pittsburgh: Imagine, 1990.

Sammartino, Bruno. "My Three Toughest Opponents." *Wrestling World*, June 1968, pp. 55–63.

"Sammartino Speaks Out." *Wrestling World*, October 1967, pp. 19–23.

Verigan, Bill. "Pedro, Bruno in Curfew Draw and All's Well." *Daily News*, October 1972, p. 78.

# Index

## Photo Credits

All photos courtesy of *Pro Wrestling Illustrated* magazine except p. 92 © AP/Worldwide.

## Series Design and Layout

Geri Giordano